Scottish Terriers

by Grace Hansen

Abdo
DOGS
Kids

abdopublishing.com

Published by Abdo Kids, a division of ABDO, P.O. Box 398166, Minneapolis, Minnesota 55439.

Copyright © 2017 by Abdo Consulting Group, Inc. International copyrights reserved in all countries. No part of this book may be reproduced in any form without written permission from the publisher.

Printed in the United States of America, North Mankato, Minnesota.

052016

092016

THIS BOOK CONTAINS RECYCLED MATERIALS

Photo Credits: Animal Photography, AP Images, iStock, Shutterstock, Thinkstock, © Grace Hansen (feat. Louie) p.4

Production Contributors: Teddy Borth, Jennie Forsberg, Grace Hansen

Design Contributors: Dorothy Toth, Laura Mitchell

Cataloging-in-Publication Data

Names: Hansen, Grace, author.

Title: Scottish terriers / by Grace Hansen.

Description: Minneapolis, MN : Abdo Kids, [2017] | Series: Dogs. Set 2 | Includes bibliographical references and index.

Identifiers: LCCN 2015959089 | ISBN 9781680805192 (lib. bdg.) | ISBN 9781680805758 (ebook) | ISBN 9781680806311 (Read-to-me ebook)

Subjects: LCSH: Scottish terrier--Juvenile literature.

Classification: DDC 636.755--dc23

LC record available at http://lccn.loc.gov/2015959089

Table of Contents

Scottish Terriers

Scottish terriers are also called "Scotties." Scotties have strong **features**, big personalities, and deep barks. They are hard to miss!

Scotties have pointed ears and tails. They have short, strong legs. Their **sturdy** bodies are covered in **wiry** hair.

Scotties come in six colors. But there are three main colors. They are black, brindle, and wheaten.

black   **brindle**   **wheaten**

Grooming

Scotties should be brushed often. Their **wiry** hair easily tangles. They need regular trips to the groomer.

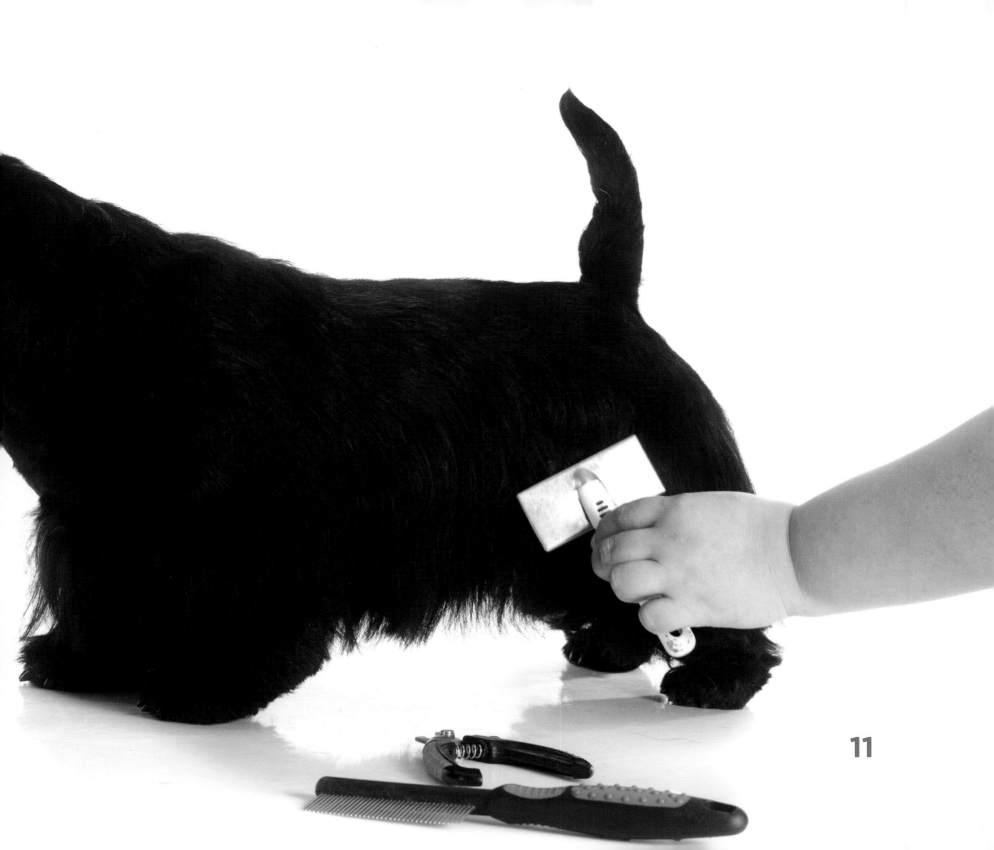

Many Scotties wear the classic cut. This includes long eyebrows and a beard. The hair is also kept long around the legs.

Walk & Play

Scotties love daily, fast walks.

They must always be leashed.

This keeps them safe.

Scotties have a strong **instinct** to chase things. They love having their toys thrown for them to run after. Their other favorite game is tug-of-war!

16

Personality

Scotties are smart and **confident**. They think their way is the right way. So, training them can be hard. Treats usually get them to work with you.

19

Scotties are never shy.
They are always loyal and
loving. But they can have
an odd way of showing it!

20

More Facts

- Four Scottish terriers have lived in the White House. Fala and Meggie belonged to Franklin D. Roosevelt. Barney and Miss Beazley were George W. Bush's Scotties.

- Scottish terriers have the second most wins at the Westminster Kennel Club Dog Show. By 2015, Scotties had won Best in Show eight times!

- Scotties have their beginnings in Scotland. Farmers and hunters used Scotties to hunt rodents, badgers, foxes, and other animals.

Glossary

confident – sure of oneself.

feature – a characteristic belonging to a thing and serving to identify it.

instinct – natural feeling.

sturdy – strongly built.

wiry – firm and stiff.

23

Index

abdokids.com

Use this code to log on to abdokids.com and access crafts, games, videos and more!

Abdo Kids Code:
DSK5192